Name It!

		an animal	something to eat	a country	something to wear	a girl's name
example	**A**	anteater	artichoke	Australia	anklets	Anna
W						
I						
N						
T						
E						
R						

EVAN-MOOR CORP., 1986   WINTER ACTIVITIES

Winter Bears At Play

1. Draw your bear in action. Use white drawing paper.

> Example: polar bear skiing
> bear cub building a snowman
> the three bears ice skating

2. Get lined paper.

> Describe your bear.
> Tell where the bear is.
> Tell what the bear is doing.
>
> Try to use good describing words.
> You may write a paragraph or a whole adventure.
> Make it interesting.

Winter Jigsaw

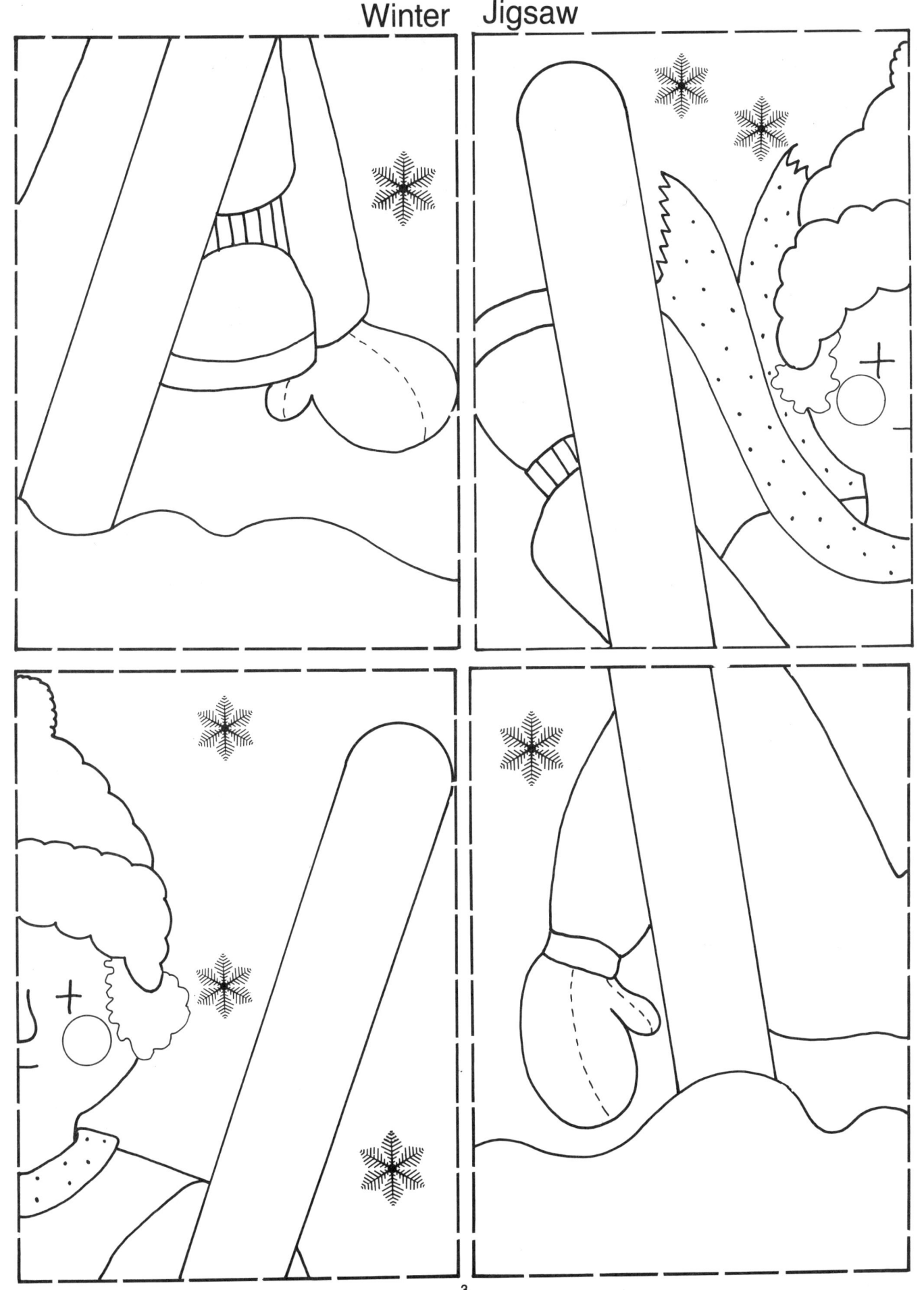

Ski Down This Snowy Hill

Try to write a winter word for each letter of the alphabet. You may need to use your dictionary.

a _____
b _____
c _____
d _____
e _____
f _____
g _____
h _____
i _____
j _____
k _____
l _____
m _____
n _____
o _____
p _____
q _____
r _____
s _____
t _____
u _____
v _____
w _____
x _____
y _____
z _____

EVAN-MOOR CORP., 1986

WINTER ACTIVITIES

Snowy Weather

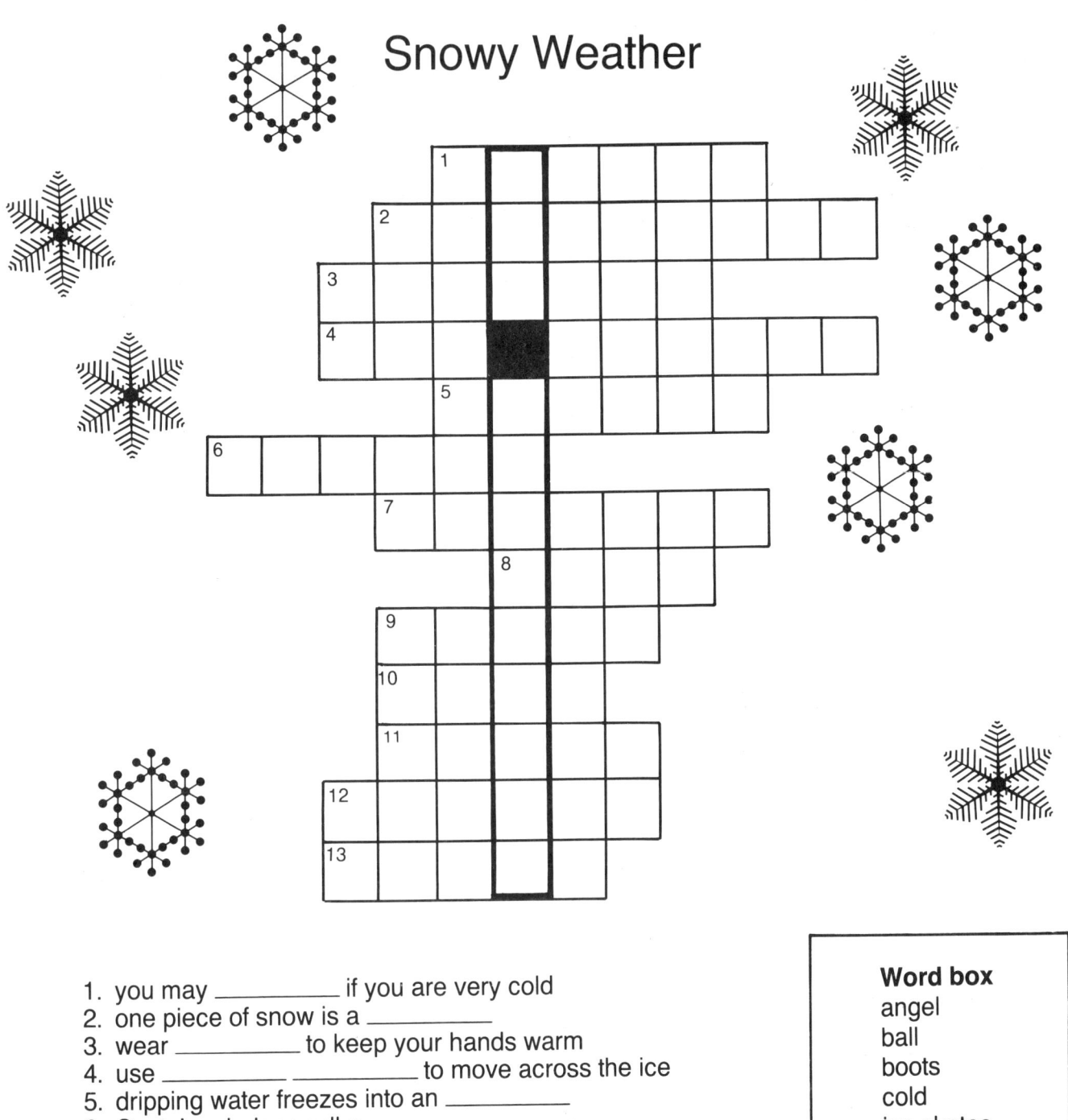

1. you may _____ if you are very cold
2. one piece of snow is a _____
3. wear _____ to keep your hands warm
4. use _____ _____ to move across the ice
5. dripping water freezes into an _____
6. Santa's reindeer pull a _____
7. a man made of snow is a _____
8. the opposite of hot is _____
9. wear _____ on your feet
10. you can throw a snow _____
11. wear a _____ around your neck
12. _____ is the coldest season of the year
13. lie down in the snow to make a snow _____

Word box
angel
ball
boots
cold
ice skates
icicle
mittens
scarf
shiver
sleigh
snowflake
snowman
winter

The mystery word is _____.

EVAN-MOOR CORP., 1986

WINTER ACTIVITIES

Finish the picture.

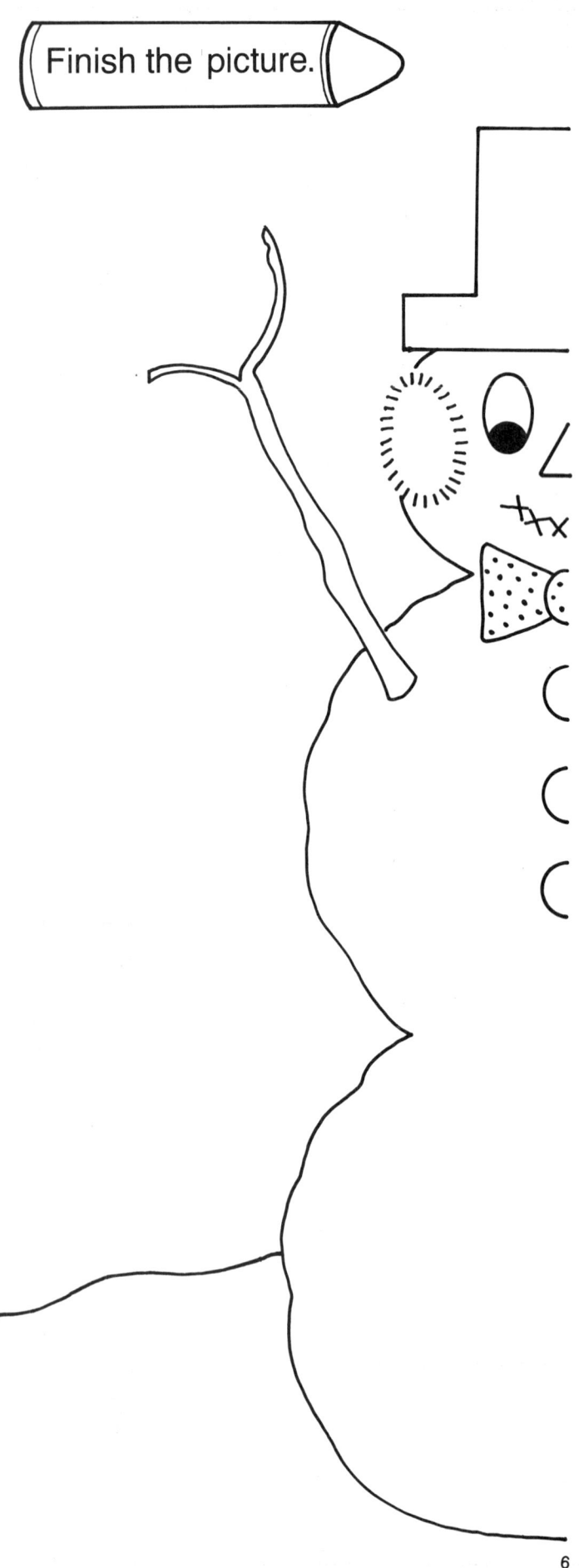

Teacher: Use this form for copying poems, writing letters or creating an original story. Paste a 7½" X 5" sheet of lined paper in the center of the border and then reproduce.

Winter Cinquain

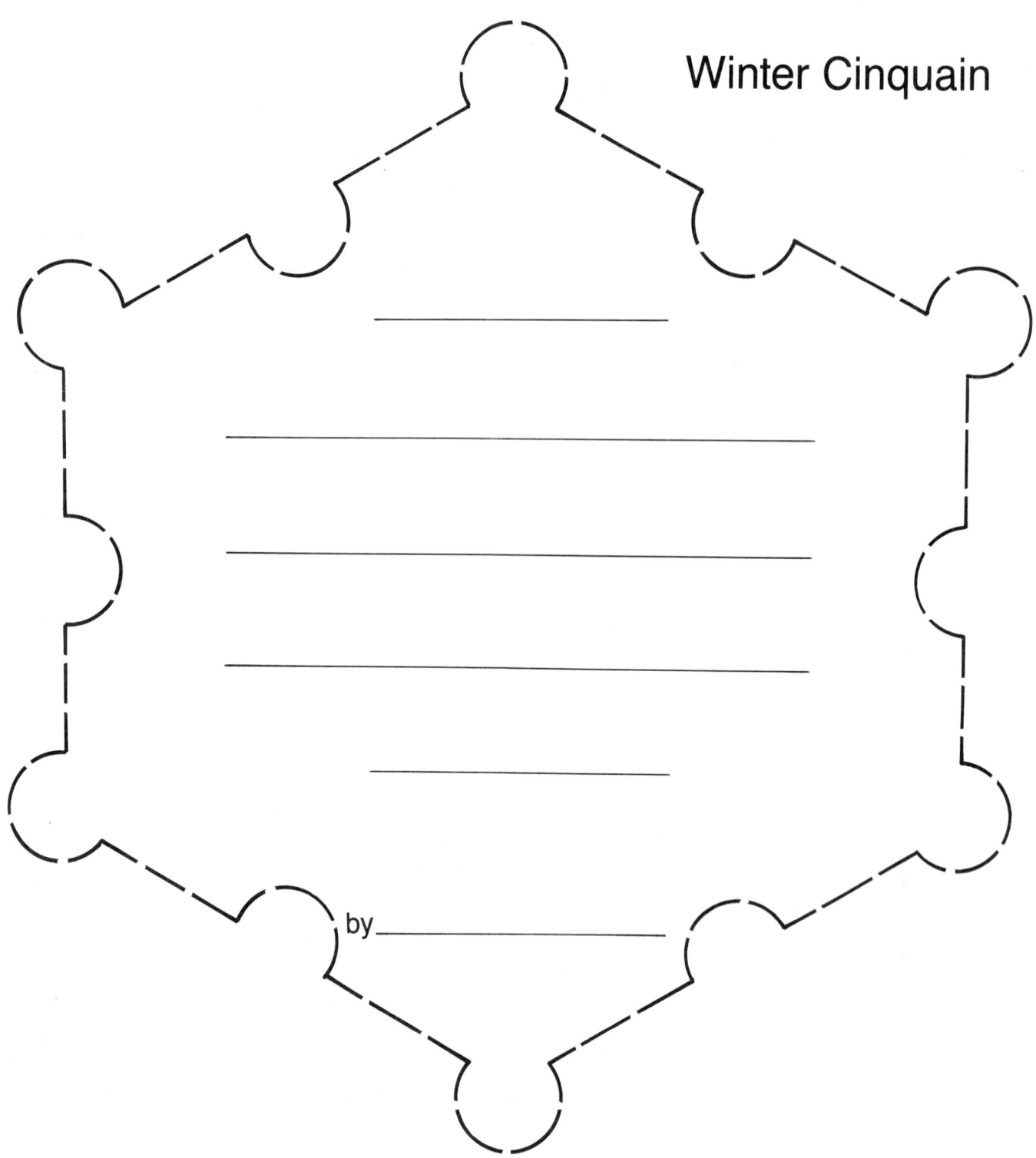

Line 1 — **one word** — title
Line 2 — **two words** — describe the title
Line 3 — **three words** — describe an action
Line 4 — **four words** — describe a feeling
Line 5 — **one word** — refer to title

Cut out the snowflake and paste it on blue paper.

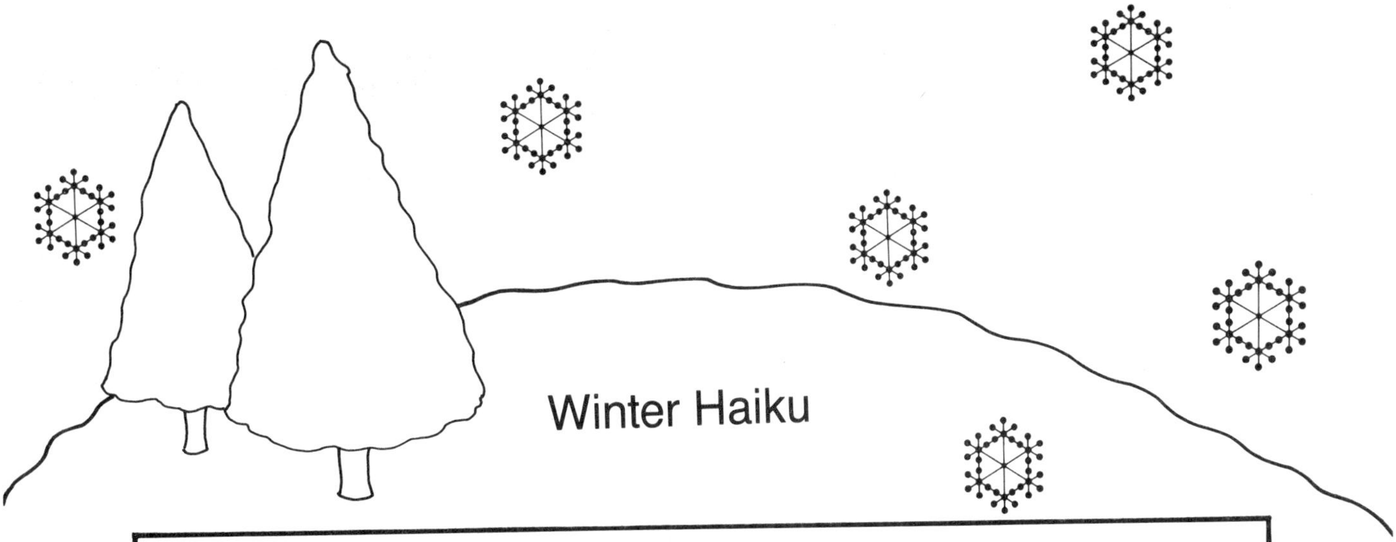

Winter Haiku

A haiku has 3 lines of 17 syllables.
It usually refers to the season or nature.
  Line 1 — 5 syllables
  Line 2 — 7 syllables
  Line 3 — 5 syllables
Start with the thought, then adjust the syllables.

Guide Bunny home!

1. Draw
2. Cut
3. Paste to lined paper
4. Write a story.

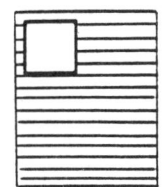

EVAN-MOOR CORP., 1986

WINTER ACTIVITIES

Winter in Alaska

Across

2. an Eskimo "jacket"
3. a winter toy used to slide across the snow
7. a pretty crystal of frozen water
9. one of the states in the U.S.A.
10. an Eskimo house made of snow blocks
12. a sealskin boot worn by Eskimos
13. a large, floating mass of ice broken off of a glacier
14. a piece of ice formed when dripping ice freezes
15. wild weather such as lightning, thunder and rain

Down

1. long strips bound to each foot for gliding across the snow
4. A group of people living in the frozen north
5. a machine for traveling over the snow
6. a large, white, hairy animal
8. an Eskimo canoe
11. a huge field of moving ice

Word Box:

Alaska	igloo	skis
Eskimos	kayak	sled
glacier	mukluk	snowflake
iceberg	parka	snowmobile
icicle	polar bear	storm

The First Christmas

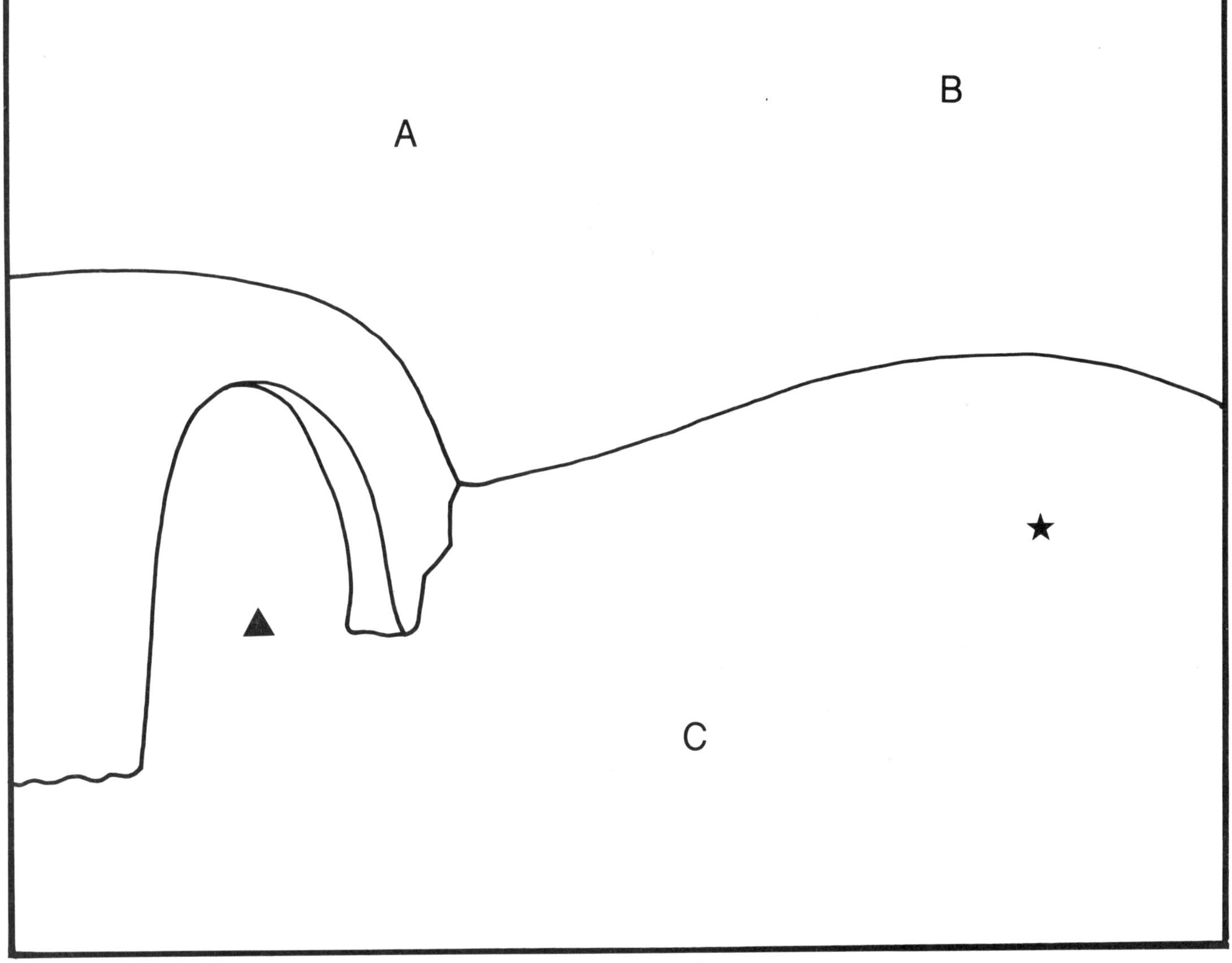

A

B

C

1. Color   2. Cut   3. Paste

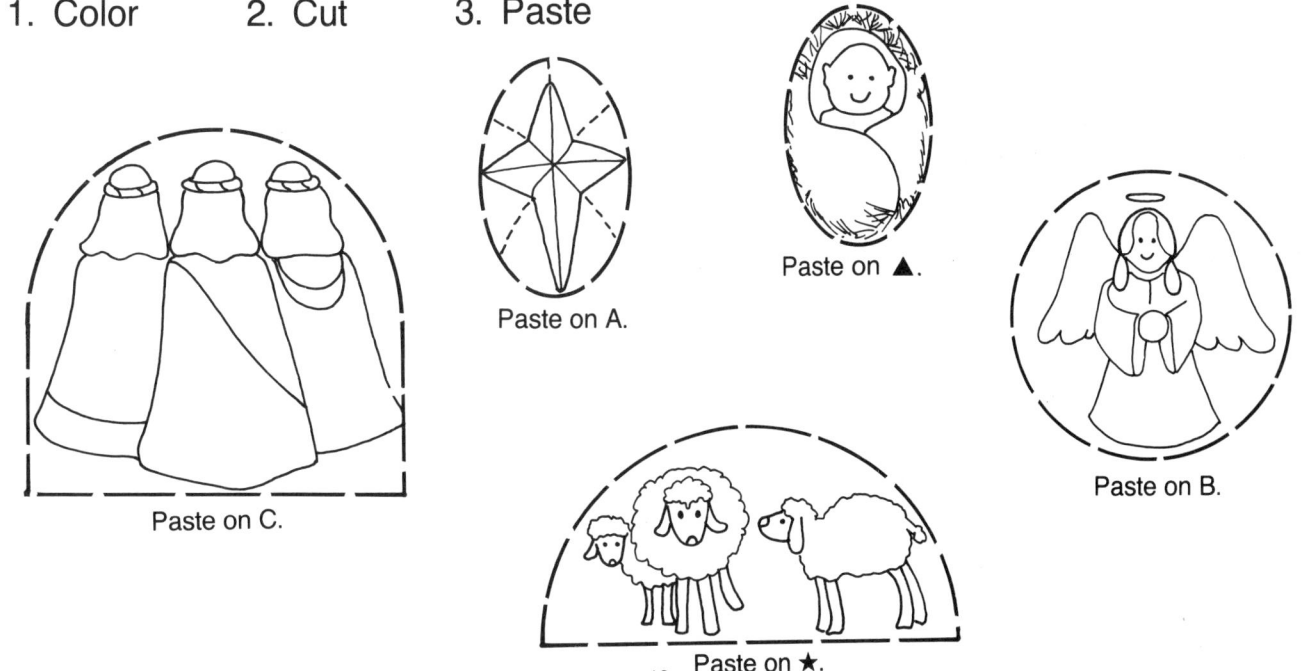

Paste on C.

Paste on A.

Paste on ▲.

Paste on B.

Paste on ★.

Riddle Time

Write your Christmas riddle on the outside.
Write and draw the answer inside.

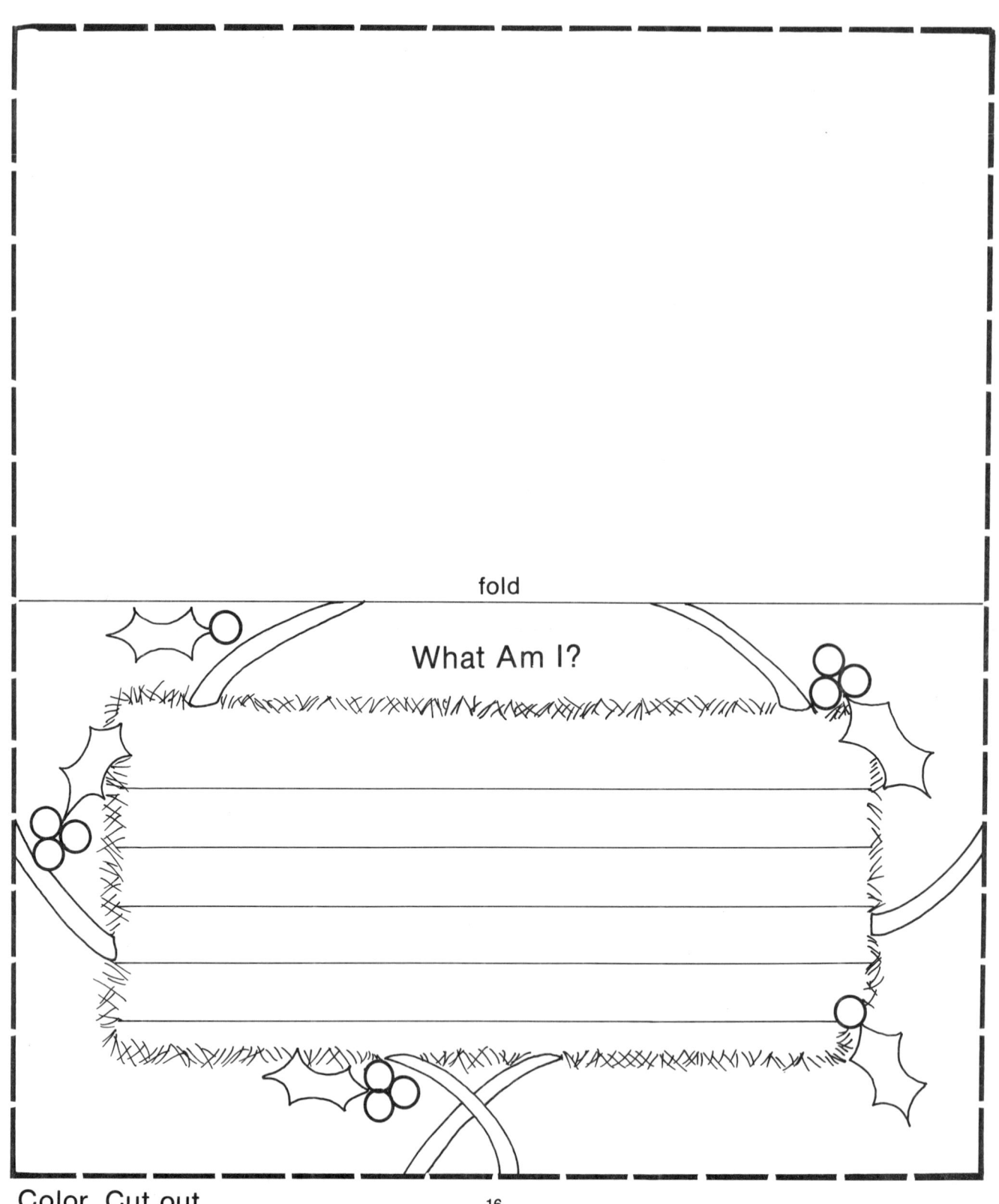

fold

What Am I?

Color. Cut out.

Connect the dots.

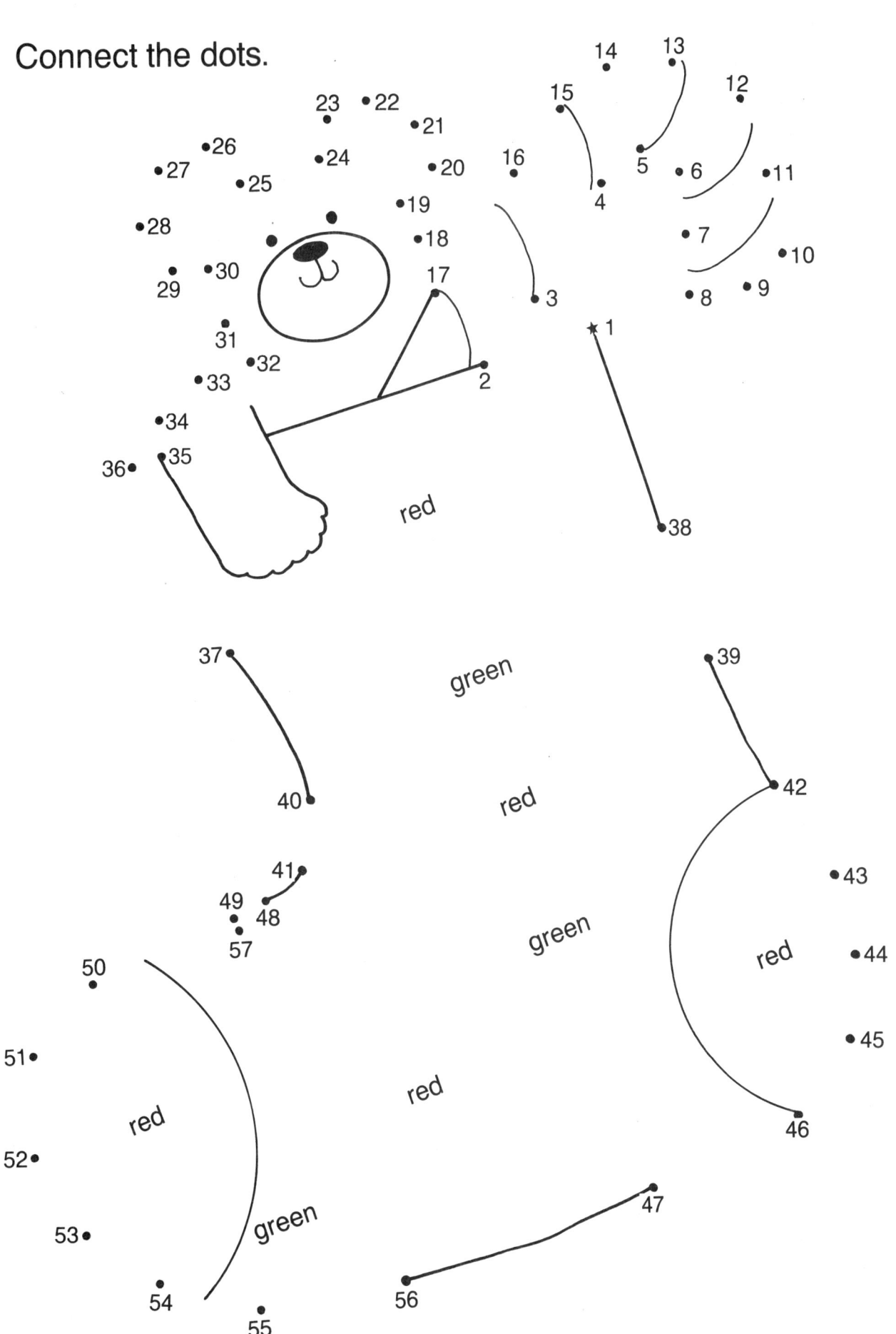

What do you see
On this Christmas tree?

Color the hidden pictures.
How many did you find? _____

Deck the Halls...

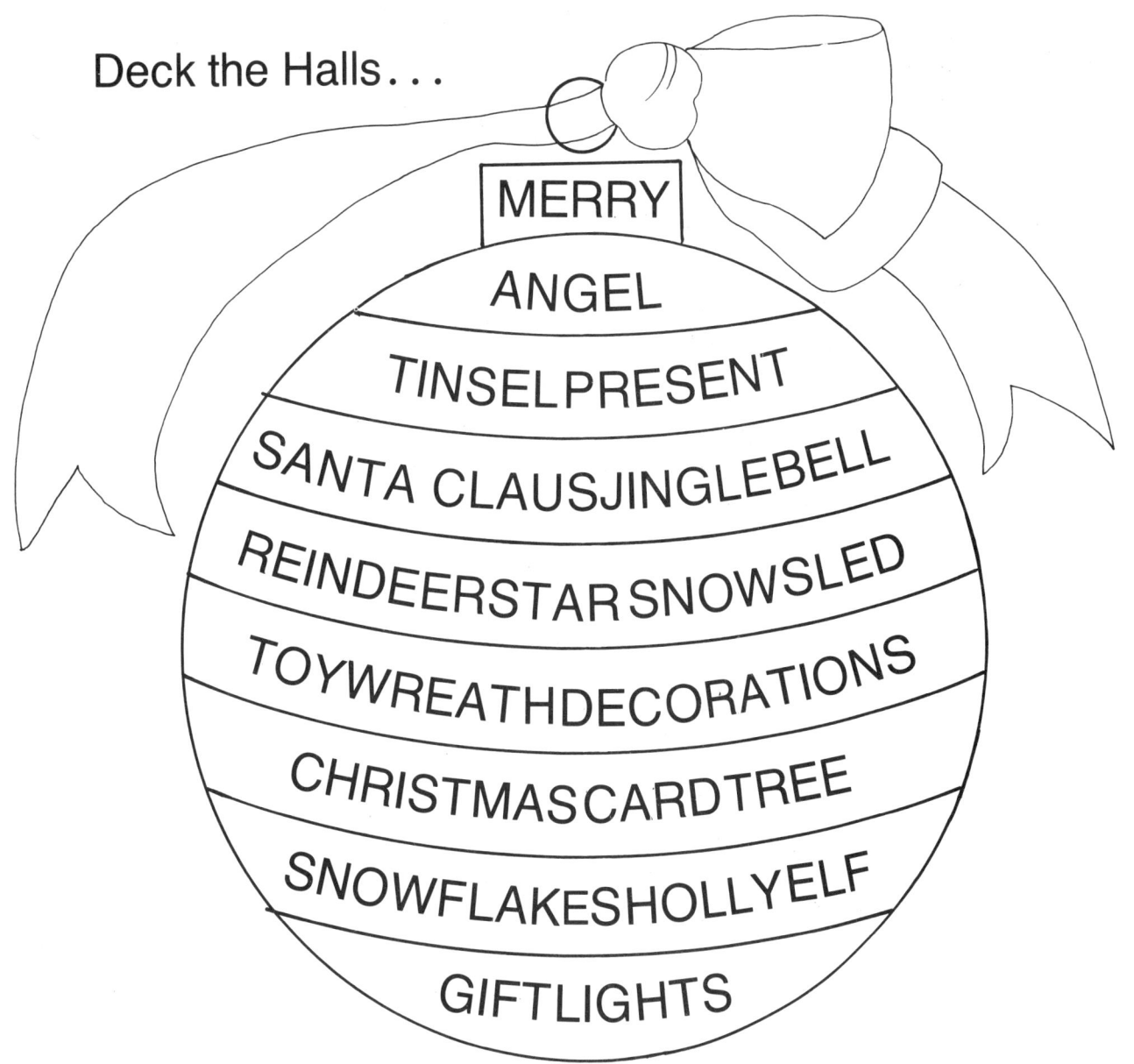

Circle and Color these words:

yellow	green	red	
MERRY	DECORATIONS GIFT LIGHTS PRESENT TINSEL TOY WREATH	ANGEL BELL CARD CHRISTMAS ELF HOLLY JINGLE	REINDEER SANTA CLAUS SLED SNOW SNOWFLAKES STAR TREE

Unscramble these Christmas Words:

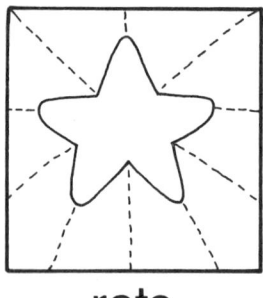  

rats   rsnpeet   dclaen

_ _ _ _   _ _ _ _ _ _ _   _ _ _ _ _ _

nStaa lusaC   reednier   nlgea

_ _ _ _ _ _ _ _ _ _   _ _ _ _ _ _ _ _   _ _ _ _ _

tarehw   tcksoign   reet

_ _ _ _ _ _   _ _ _ _ _ _ _ _   _ _ _ _

angel	star	present
candle	wreath	reindeer
tree	stocking	Santa Claus

Silent Night, Christmas Night

```
R E I N D E E R C E L E B R A T E
S W G I F T Y S A N T A C L A U S
T R S I S E N N F R X N A B O H I
A E D L N T M O I E L G R M P P L
R A T M E G O W R L B E D L A O E
E T I R C I E C P T N L O O C I N
K H N H E Q G R K K H D P V K N T
C F S Y C E G H B I U P J E A S N
P R E S E N T V O R N A O N G E I
E G L I G H T S T S E G S L E T G
P A C K C H R I S T M A S R E T H
F E A S T O I J W F O O D T Q I T
H C A N D L E S L L A M B B U A Z
C O O K Y L D E C O R A T I O N S
S H A R E Y M I S T L E T O E Y A
J I N G L E B E L L S C R E C H E
```

ANGEL
CANDLES
CARD
CELEBRATE
CHIMNEY
CHRISTMAS
COOKY
CRECHE
DECORATIONS
ELF
FIR
FEAST

FOOD
GIFT
GINGERBREAD BOY
HOLLY
JINGLE BELLS
LAMB
LIGHTS
LOVE
MISTLETOE
NORTH POLE
PACK
PACKAGE
PRESENT

POINSETTA
REINDEER
RUDOLPH
SANTA CLAUS
SHARE
SILENT NIGHT
SLEIGH
SNOW
STAR
STOCKING
TINSEL
TREE
WREATH

EVAN-MOOR CORP., 1986   WINTER ACTIVITIES

Once upon a Christmas Time

Write a paragraph describing a favorite Christmas memory. Then illustrate your paragraph.

Here are some ideas to help you get started.

☐ Your Own Memories
1. My Earliest Christmas Memory
2. The Best Part of Christmas
3. My favorite Christmas Gift

☐ A Friend's Christmas Memory
Interview a friend or relative, then write.
1. _____'s Favorite Christmas
   _{name}
2. Christmas When I Was A Child
3. Christmas in _____
   _{country}

☐ The First Christmas
Re-tell the story of the first Christmas experience from the point of view of:
1. The Wise Men
2. Mary and Joseph
3. A Poor Shepherd Boy

EVAN-MOOR CORP., 1986 WINTER ACTIVITIES

Stocking Surprises

1. Place this page on a sheet of lined paper.
2. Cut out the stocking and the lined paper at the same time.
3. Write about what you would like to find in your Christmas stocking.
4. Glue your story and stocking together at the top.

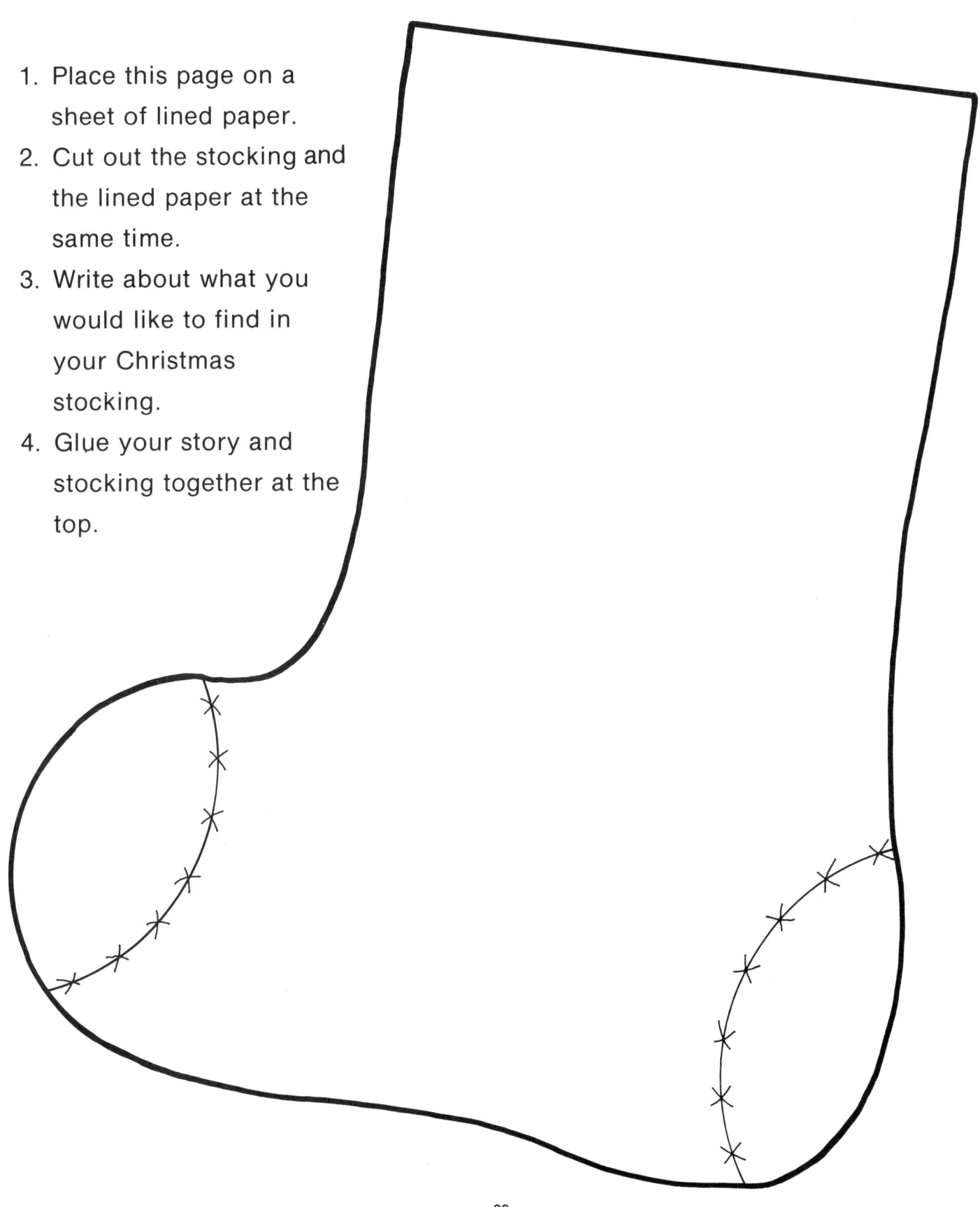

Follow the directions below to finish this picture.

___ Draw a large, green Christmas tree in the blue box.
___ Put these ornaments on the tree:
   ___ a large yellow star on top
   ___ 9 colorful balls
   ___ 5 red and white candy canes
   ___ a long string of lights
___ Make five beautiful presents under the tree.
___ Make the fireplace look like reddish-brown brick.
___ Draw three stockings hanging on the fireplace. Make each one different.
___ Put a large wreath with a big red bow over the fireplace
___ Make a kitten sleeping on a rug in front of the fireplace.

1. Choose a story beginning.   2. Paste it to a sheet of paper.   3. Write

Santa's elves are very upset. A terrible disaster has happened in the toy factory.

Christmas Eve is over. Now Santa Claus will...

Getting presents is always fun, but to me the best part of Christmas is...

Mrs. Claus has been busy all year. It is her responsibility to...

Color the boxes to find the mystery picture.

1	milk	tomato	pepper	pie	jellybean	bread	fish	cake	chicken
2	cloud	rain	thunder	pencil	teddy bear	chalk	wind	snow	sunshine
3	cap	scarf	glove	sock	boot	slipper	dress	shirt	belt
4	toes	knee	nose	sled	chin	eye	lips	finger	arm
5	chair	table	plane	bird	blimp	marble	jet	bed	stool
6	cabbage	banana	lime	grape	pineapple	apple	pear	peach	spinach
7	barn	rose	ball	tulip	daisy	daffodil	jumprope	geranium	shed
8	red	top	yellow	blue	doll	purple	orange	kite	brown
9	Jo Ellen	Anna	Bill	Marilyn	Lucy	Olive	Earl	Ginny	Joy
10	Texas	New York	Idaho	Oregon	tractor	Iowa	Ohio	Utah	Nevada
11	under	over	into	above	fir tree	below	next	after	by
12	elf	fairy	pixie	juice	milk	lemonade	giant	unicorn	ghost

Row 1– Make all candy green.
Row 2– Color all things you can draw with green.
Row 3– Make everything you put on your feet green.
Row 4– Color everything on your face green.
Row 5– Make things that fly green.
Row 6– Make all fruit green.
Row 7– Color all flowers green.
Row 8– Make all color words green.
Row 9– Color all names green.
Row 10– Color all machines brown.
Row 11– Color plants brown.
Row 12– Color things you drink blue.
★ Color all toys on this page red.

Use the code to find the answers.

a-1	e-4	k-7	r-10	u-13
c-2	h-5	n-8	s-11	y-15
d-3	i-6	o-9	t-12	z-16

Where do gingerbread men sleep?

| 13 | 8 | 3 | 4 | 10 | | 2 | 9 | 9 | 7 | 6 | 4 | | 11 | 5 | 4 | 4 | 12 | 11 |

Why does Rudolph need an umbrella?

| 5 | 4 | 11 | | 1 |
| | | , | | |

| 10 | 4 | 6 | 8 | 3 | 4 | 4 | 10 |

A Recipe For the Perfect Christmas

Think about it:

    What ingredients make Christmas special for your family?
        people   activities   food
        places   decorations   memories
        _____   _____   _____
    How do these mix together to make Christmas into a wonderful day?

Now...write your "recipe."

_____'s Recipe for a Perfect Christmas

Ingredients:
_____   _____
_____   _____
_____   _____
_____   _____

Directions:
_____
_____
_____
_____
_____
_____
_____
_____
_____

Start at ★.

Count by 2s.

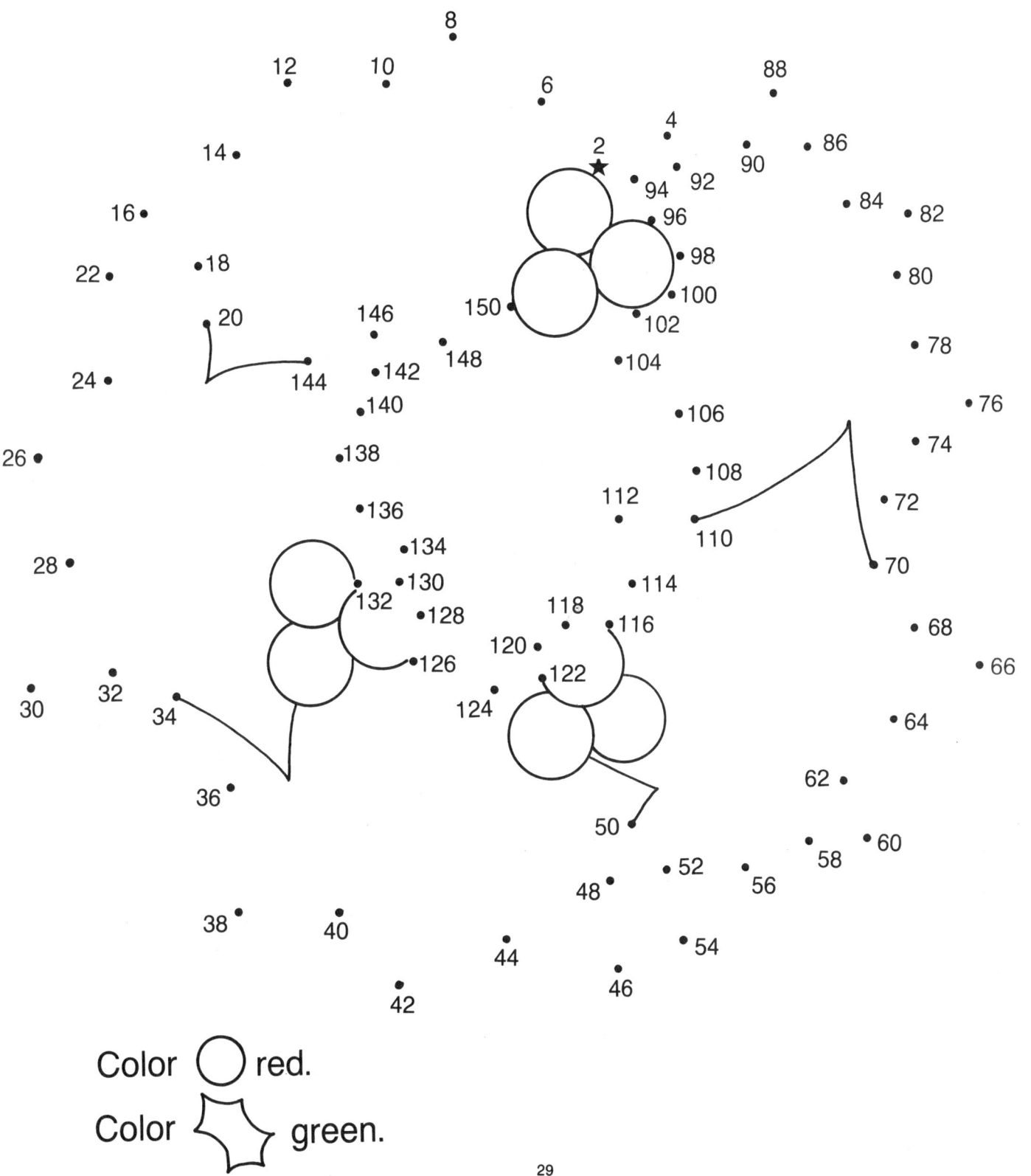

Color ◯ red.
Color ✦ green.

Gingerbread House

1. Color   2. Cut   3. Fold   4. Paste

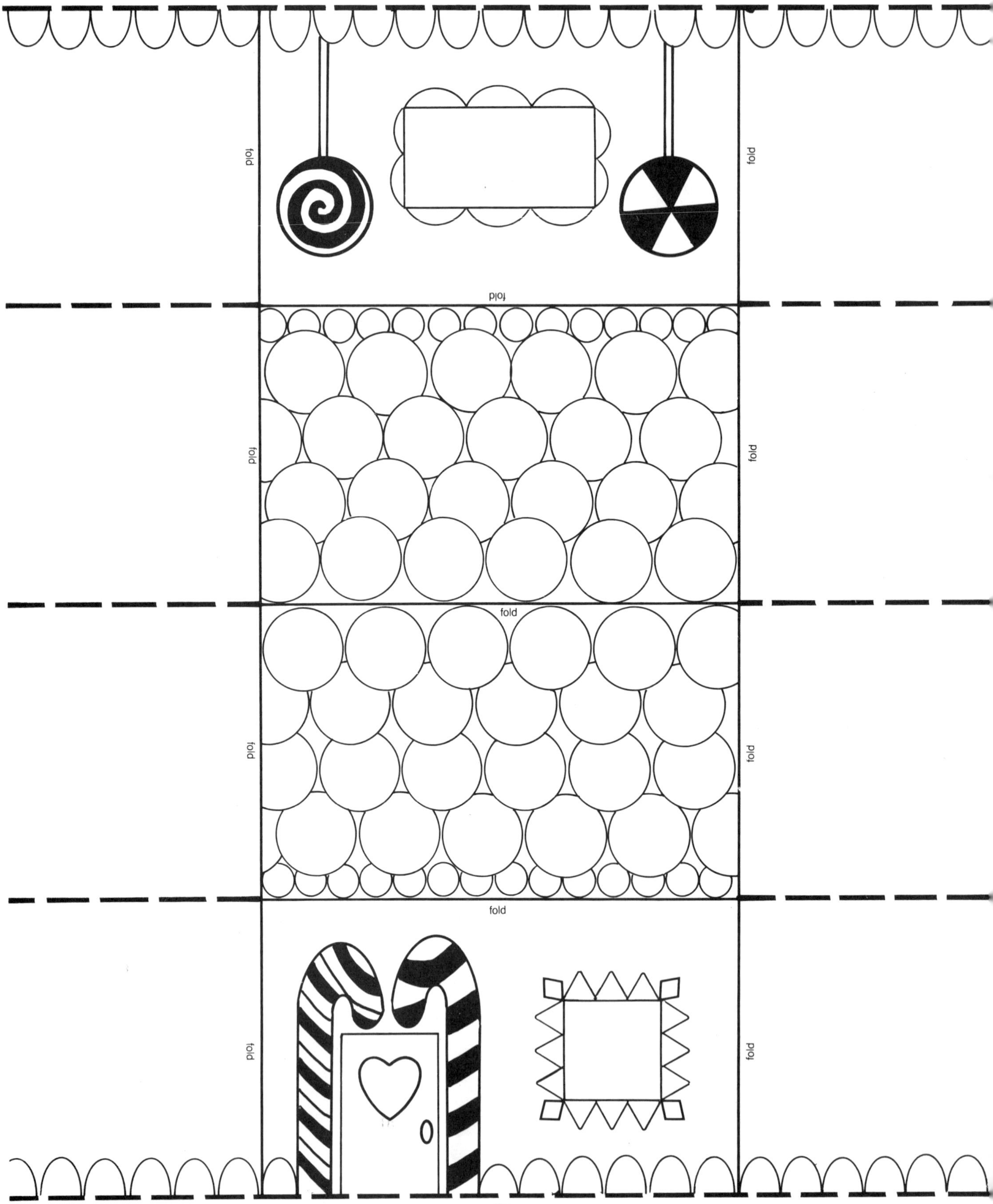

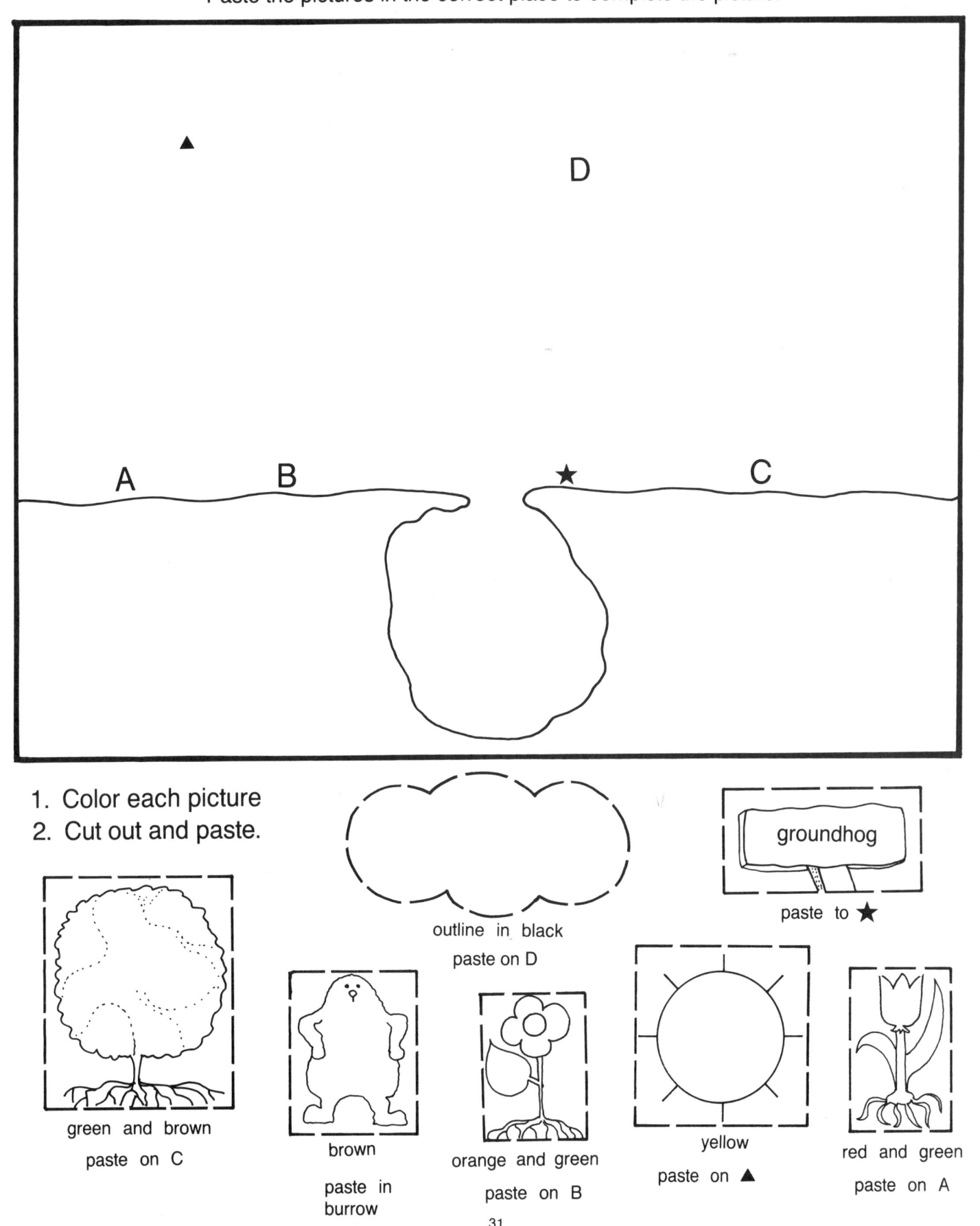

Words that Describe

Weather Watch
List the words that decribe weather:

Feelings
List emotion words here:

afraid · fainthearted · pleasant
alarmed · foggy · rainy
apprehensive · foul · shy
balmy · frightened · skittish
breezy · gusty · stormy
bright · hazy · sunshiny
brisk · inclement · terrified
cautious · jumpy · timid
cloudy · nervous · uneasy
cloudless · overcast · upset
dismayed · panicky · wary
windy

Add one word of your own to each list.

Catch the Knave of Hearts and rescue the Queen's Tarts

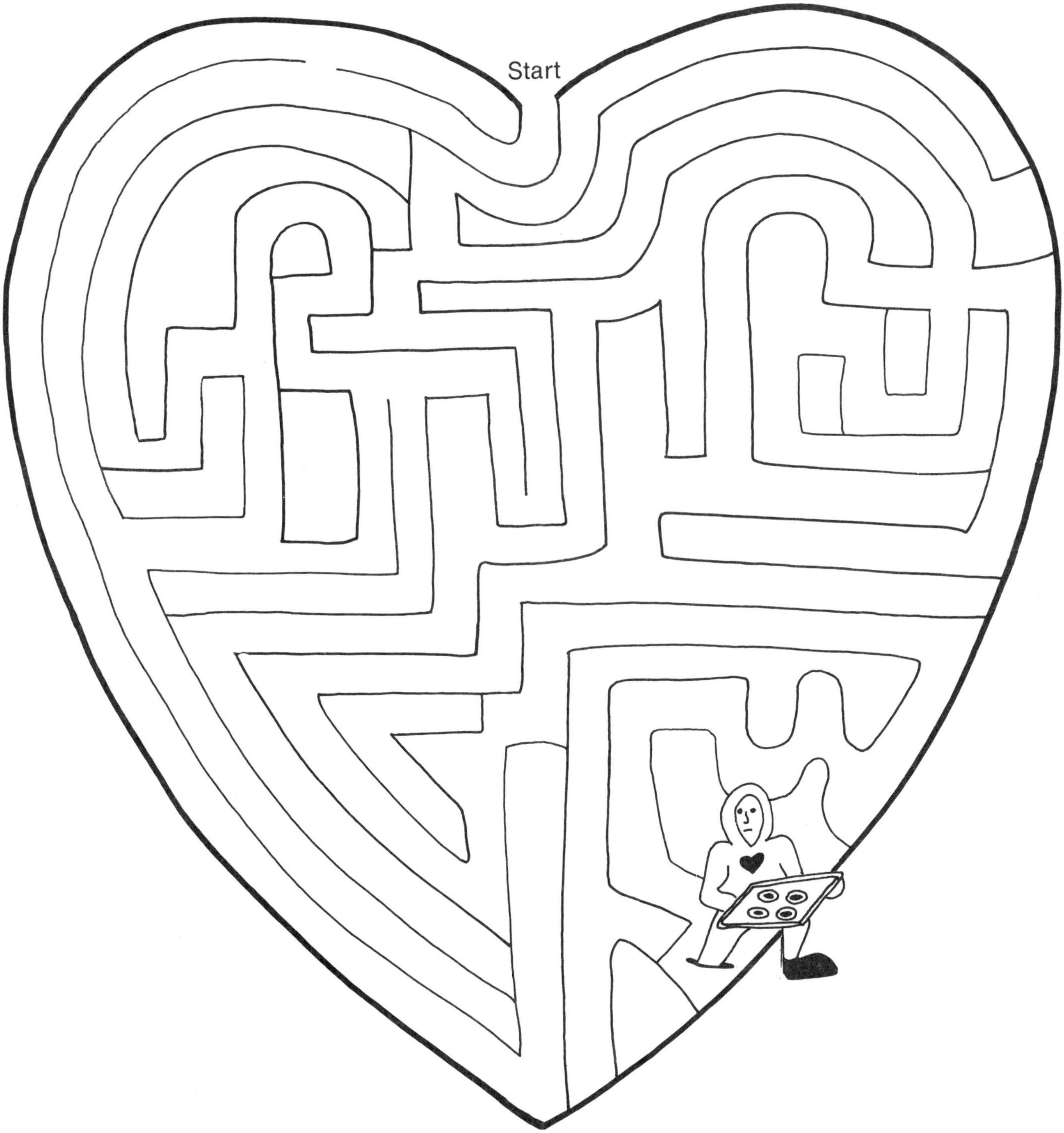

Start

A Holiday Headband

1. Color
2. Cut on ....
3. Paste or staple front and back together.

Happy Valentines Day from Your Teacher

Love Bugs

Create a "heart-y" insect to carry your Valentine wishes to special friends.

You will need:

- tongue depressor for a body
- pipe cleaners for the antennae
- pink, red, white scraps for hearts

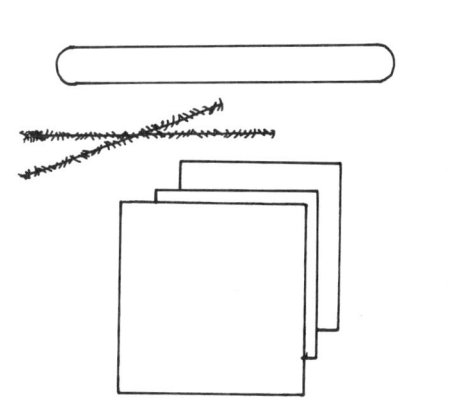

Ideas you might use:

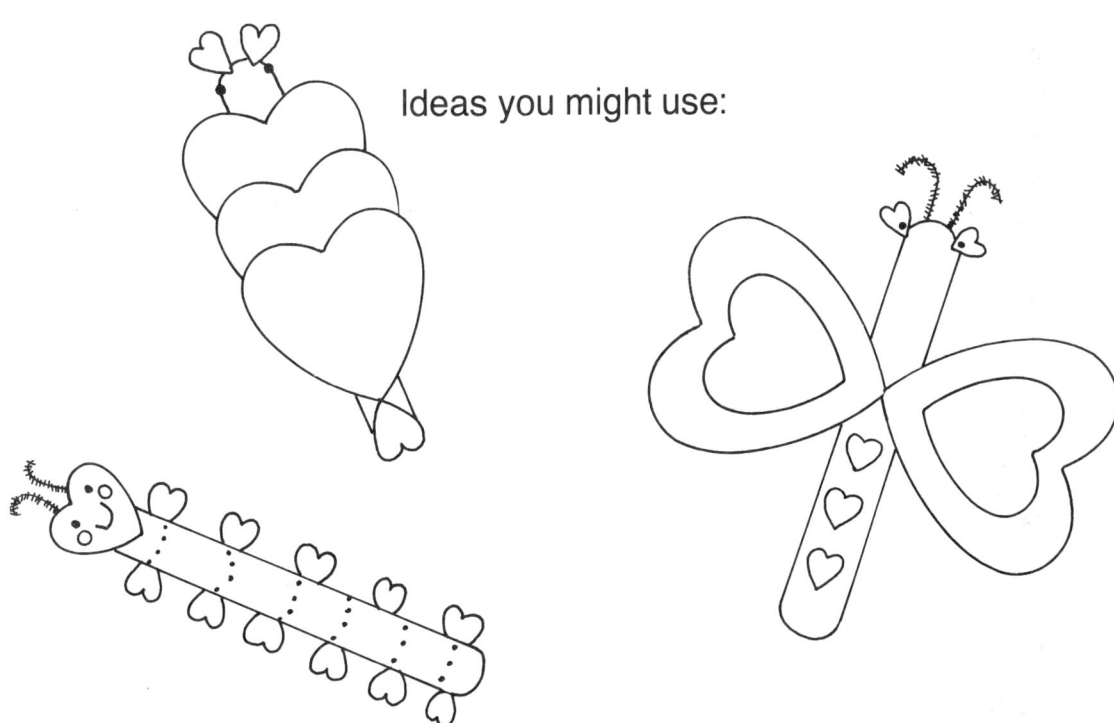

Now...
   Cut out your own hearts and set your imagination to work.

Valentine Messages

Use the code to solve the riddles.

A-26	F-21	L-15	Q-10	V-5
B-25	G-20	M-14	R-9	W-4
C-24	H-19	N-13	S-8	X-3
D-23	I-18	O-12	T-7	Y-2
E-22	J-17	P-11	U-6	Z-1
	K-16			

What did the pig write to his sweetheart?

19·12·20·8   26·13·23   16·18·8   8·22·8
_ _ _ _   _ _ _   _ _ _ _ _ _

What did the owl write to her sweetheart?

12·4·15   26·15·4·26·2·8   25·22
_ _ _   _ _ _ _ _ _   _ _

2·12·6·9   5·26·15·22·13·7·18·13·22
_ _ _ _   _ _ _ _ _ _ _ _ _

What did the bee say to his sweetheart?

2·12·6   9·22   26   19·12·13·22·2
_ _ _ , _ _   _   _ _ _ _ _

12·21   26   5·26·15·22·13·7·18·13·22
_ _   _   _ _ _ _ _ _ _ _ _!

Mend These Broken Hearts

Select the three words that go together to create a set. Write the words in the correct heart. You may need to use a dictionary!

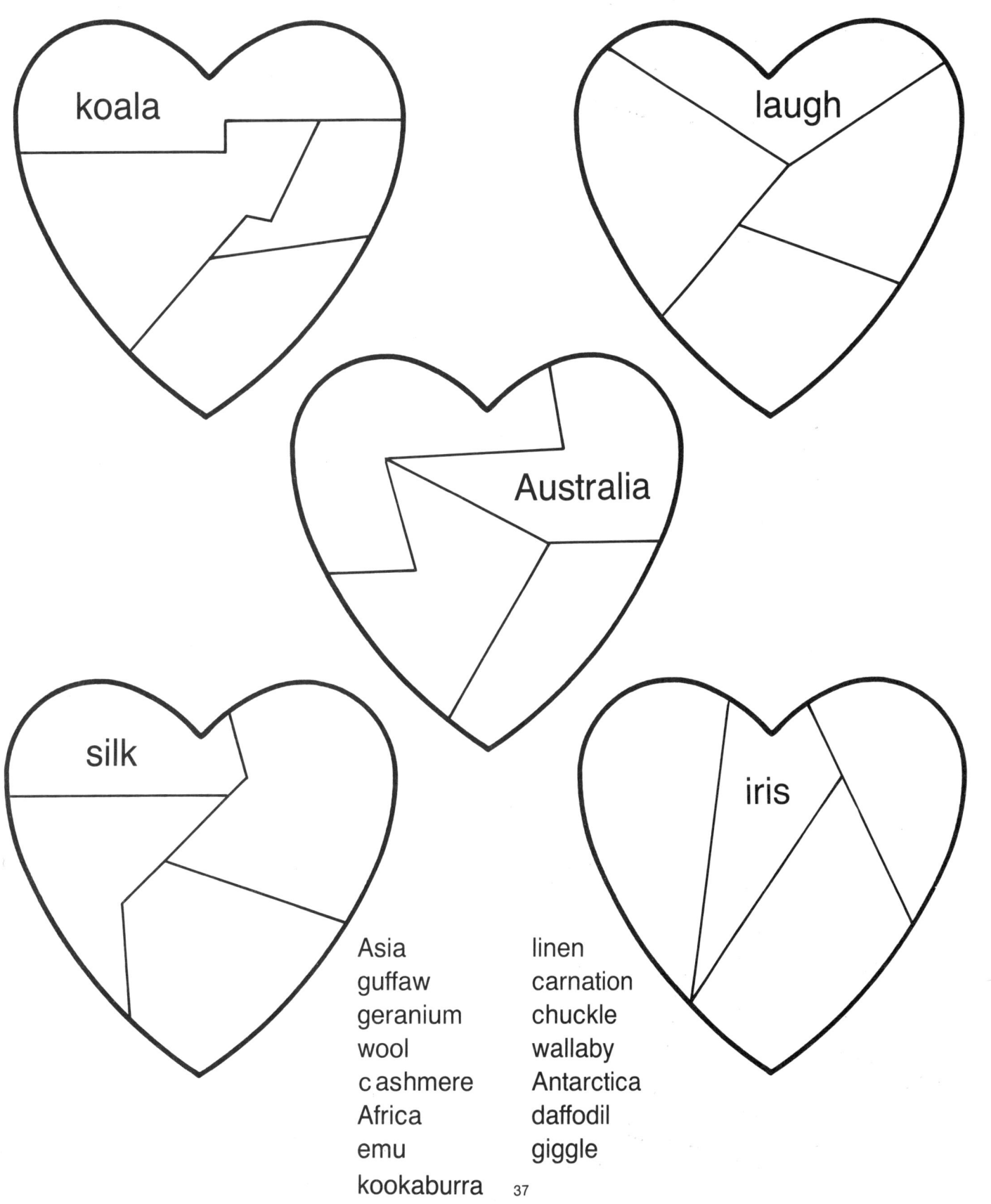

koala

laugh

Australia

silk

iris

Asia
guffaw
geranium
wool
cashmere
Africa
emu
kookaburra

linen
carnation
chuckle
wallaby
Antarctica
daffodil
giggle

Cut out on the _ _ _ _ lines.
Paste the puzzle together on a sheet of blue paper.
Color the Valentine.

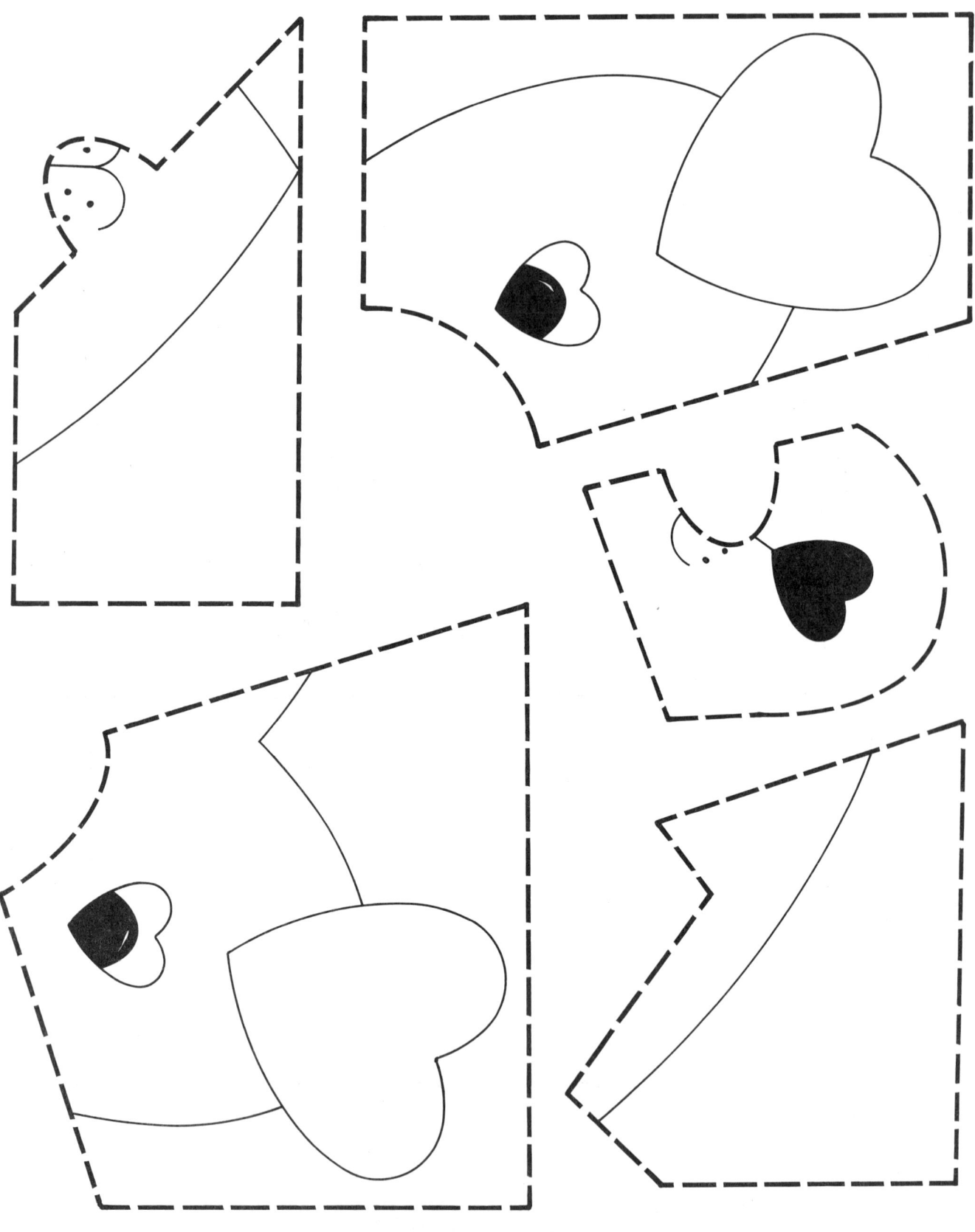

Write Your Own Valentine Rhymes

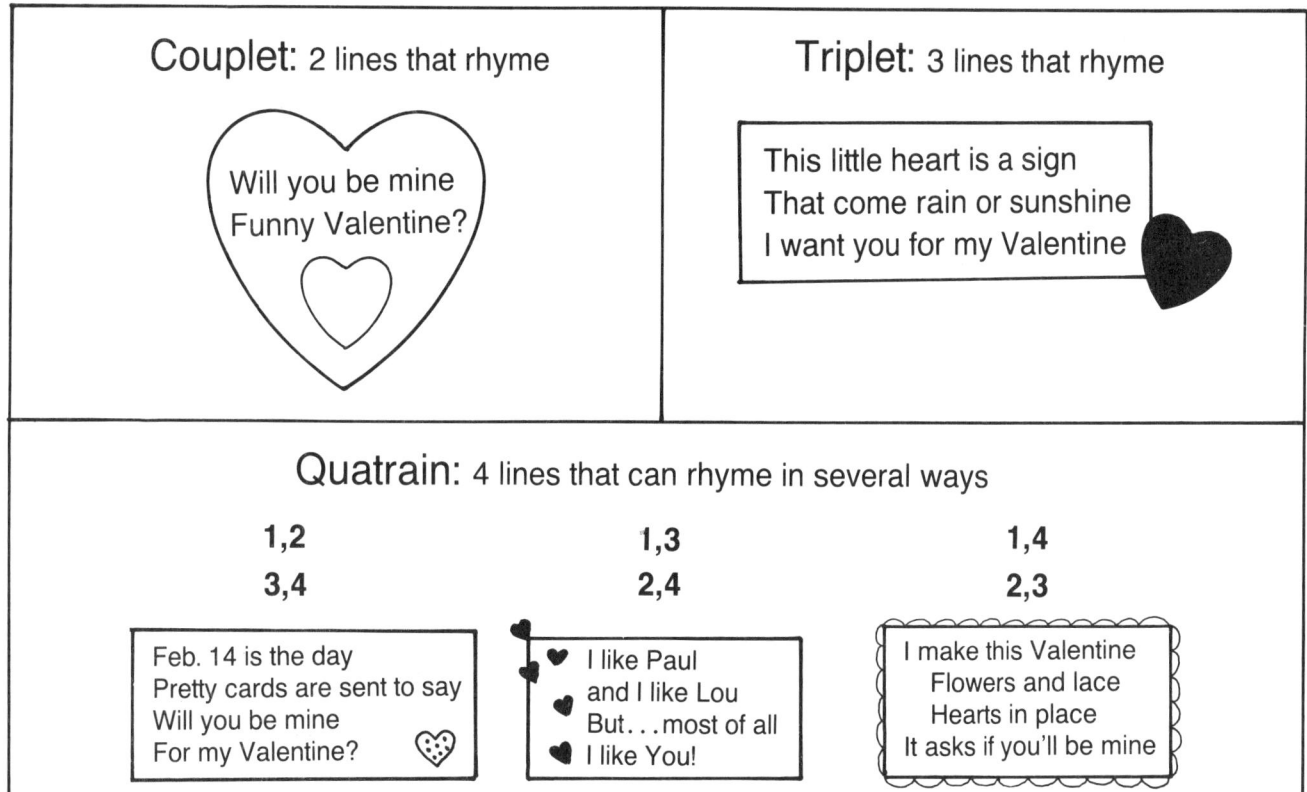

Couplet: 2 lines that rhyme

Will you be mine
Funny Valentine?

Triplet: 3 lines that rhyme

This little heart is a sign
That come rain or sunshine
I want you for my Valentine

Quatrain: 4 lines that can rhyme in several ways

1,2   1,3   1,4
3,4   2,4   2,3

Feb. 14 is the day
Pretty cards are sent to say
Will you be mine
For my Valentine?

I like Paul
and I like Lou
But...most of all
I like You!

I make this Valentine
Flowers and lace
Hearts in place
It asks if you'll be mine

Create your own rhyme.

Give it to a special friend.

Find the Valentine Message

1. month after January
2. blossoms like daffodils
3. happy; cheerful
4. sweets like chocolate
5. special friendship; affection
6. a greeting sent through the mail
7. cup-shaped flowers
8. the shape of Valentines
9. a pal; someone you enjoy being with
10. a celebration
11. mix red and white to get _____
12. a short letter
13. a delicate edging used on clothes for decoration

What is the secret message?

_____

Connect the dots to find this famous American.

Who am I? _____

41

EVAN-MOOR CORP., 1986 WINTER ACTIVITIES

Count by 2's to find this famous American.

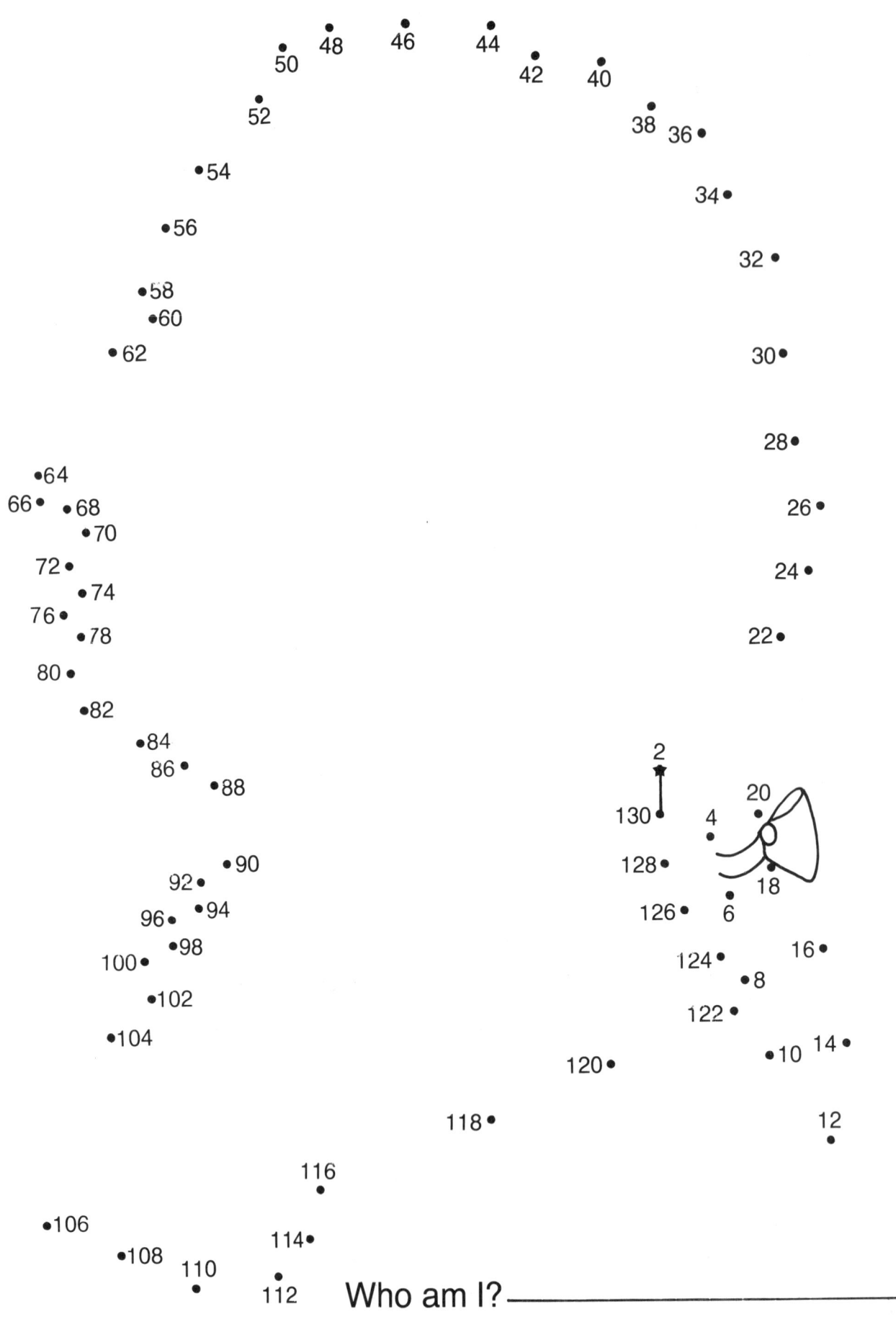

Who am I? _____

George Washington and Abraham Lincoln

Write these facts next to the correct picture:

1st president of the USA
16th president of the USA
called "Honest Abe"
called "Father of his Country"
was a farmer and surveyor
was a rail-splitter and lawyer
born in Virginia on Feb. 22, 1732
born in Kentucky on Feb. 12, 1809

his family plantation was called Mt. Vernon
he grew up in a log cabin
married Martha Dandridge
married Mary Todd
General in the Revolutionary War
President during the Civil War
shot and killed in 1865
died of illness in 1799

1. Cut out a picture.   2. Paste it to lined paper.   3. Write.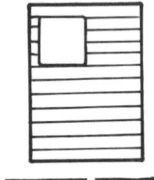

Search For The Presidents

```
K M E N W I L S O N E M A C L
H A C I A F T Y L E R C S L G
A D A M S M O N R O E K H E A
R I R E H E T R O P D I J V R
D S T V I E N A D R O N A E F
I O E A N N I H Y A T L C L I
N N R N G R E G O L L E K A E
G F F S T A F T R W O Y S N L
P I O N O L S O N A E R O D D
I L L I N C O L N S N R N I E
E L W X R E A G A N A T I N A
R M H O O V E R J O H N S O N
C O I N O A R T T R U M A N M
E R S U S N B U C H A N A N U
J E F F E R S O N A R T H U R
A L D O V A N B U R E N E A R
K E N N E D Y I H A Y E S H Y
E M I L L E R C O O L I D G E
G I L L T H A R R I S O N S O
```

___ Adams
___ Arthur
___ Buchanan
___ Carter
___ Cleveland
___ Coolidge
___ Eisenhower
___ Fillmore
___ Ford

___ Garfield
___ Grant
___ Harding
___ Harrison
___ Hayes
___ Hoover
___ Jackson
___ Jefferson
___ Johnson

___ Kennedy
___ Lincoln
___ Madison
___ McKinley
___ Monroe
___ Nixon
___ Pierce
___ Polk
___ Reagan

___ Roosevelt
___ Taft
___ Taylor
___ Truman
___ Tyler
___ VanBuren
___ Washington
___ Wilson

AN-MOOR CORP., 1986

WINTER ACTIVITIES

A Visit to Washington D.C.

Poll 20 people.
Ask them the following two questions.
Record their answers on graphs A and B.

A. Have you ever visited Washington, D.C.?

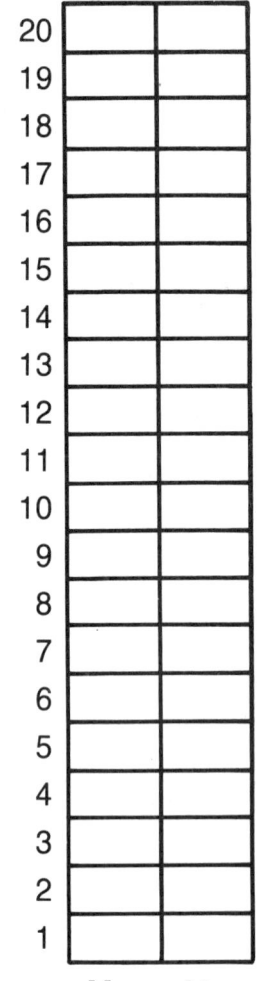

B. Did you see any of these buildings?

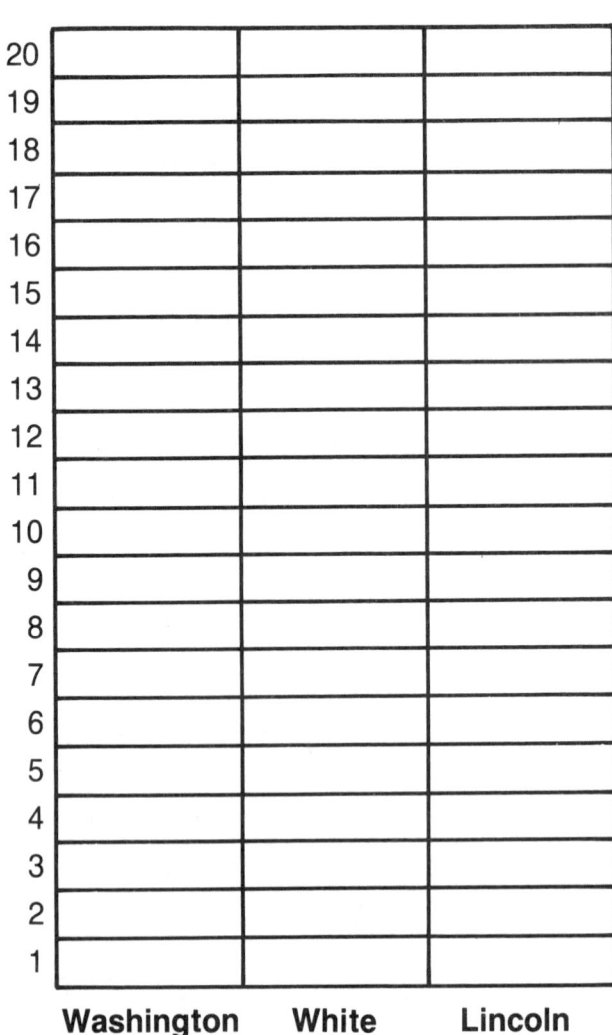

A Report

★★

_____

President's Name

1. Read about the president you chose.
2. Write one or two paragraphs for each part.
3. Illustrate your report.

★★

Part 1 — Childhood
- Tell when and where he was born.
- Describe his childhood.
    What did he do?
    What was his family like?
    Did he have any special dreams for when he grew up?

Part 2 — Before Becoming President
- What types of jobs did he do?
- Tell about his wife and children.

Part 3 — The Presidential Years
- Tell when he was president and for how long.
- Describe how he was chosen to be President.
- What were some of the important events that happened while he was president?

Part 4 — Why do we remember this president?

Use the code to decipher the names of these famous American sights. Paste the correct picture by each name.

★★

```
1  2  3  4  5  6  7  8  9  10 11 12 13 14 15 16 17 18 19 20 21 22 23 24 25 26
A  B  C  D  E  F  G  H  I  J  K  L  M  N  O  P  Q  R  S  T  U  V  W  X  Y  Z
```

3 1 16 9 20 15 12
— — — — — — —
2 21 9 12 4 9 14 7
— — — — — — — —

13 20.
— —
18 21 19 8 13 15 18 5
— — — — — — — —

12 9 14 3 15 12 14
— — — — — — —
13 5 13 15 18 9 1 12
— — — — — — — —

23 1 19 8 9 14 7 20 15 14
— — — — — — — — — —
13 15 14 21 13 5 14 20
— — — — — — — —

48

EVAN-MOOR CORP., 1986

WINTER ACTIVITIE